Young Heroes

Dana White

Illustrations by Derrick Williams

1 2 3 4 5 6 7 8 9 10
ISBN 0-8250-4965-7

Walch Publishing
P. O. Box 658 • Portland, Maine 04104-0658
walch.com
Printed in the United States of America

Table of Contents

Introduction

Ask 12 people to name their hero. You will get a dozen different answers. Someone might say a pop star. The pop star is admired. That is one kind of hero.

A great warrior is another kind of hero. At 16, Alexander the Great led his first army and founded his first city. He was another kind of a hero.

Running Eagle was a great warrior. She also had great courage. She followed her own path, even though at first people thought she was wrong. Her story is in this book.

The story of Albert Smith is here, too. At 15, he left home and joined a group of special soldiers who helped the United States during World War II. Iqbal Masih fought with words to free thousands of child slaves. Samantha Smith had the courage to speak for peace. So did Gerson Perez. At 15, he was nominated for the Nobel Peace Prize. Ruby Bridges walked through hatred and did not falter.

What these people did was heroic. And they were kids. They were too young to vote or drive. But their actions changed the world.

Do you think kids can't do important things? That adults will not listen? Think again. Get ready to meet some young heroes who did some very important things.

Albert Smith, Navajo Code Talker

In 1942, Albert Smith was 15. He lived on a Navajo reservation near Gallup, New Mexico. The United States was fighting World War II. And news from the Pacific Theater—one area of fighting—was terrible.

The American Army had surrendered at Bataan in the Philippine Islands. It was the largest American army surrender in history. More than 70,000 American and Filipino soldiers were taken prisoners of war by the Japanese. They were force-marched out of Bataan to be assigned to other prison camps. The Bataan Death March was 60 double-time miles of blistering heat. There was little food and water. Many would not finish the journey.

That was when Marine Corps

recruiters came to Albert Smith's reservation. They wanted men fluent in both English and Navajo. For decades, government boarding schools had a strict rule for American Indian students: *do not speak your language*. Now the government wanted Navajo to speak Navajo! Albert "advanced his age a little" to enlist in the Marines. He left the reservation for basic training.

After basic training, Albert joined a special group—the Code Talkers. These were Navajo soldiers who created a code based on their language. It worked like this: Some English words were translated into Navajo. Other times, the first letter of the English translation of a Navajo word would spell out names or places. There were 411 signs. They would be memorized and used to send vital military messages.

It was difficult. Code Talkers had to translate between English and Navajo instantly. One mistake could cost thousands of lives. But it worked. Navy intelligence officers spent three weeks trying to figure out one coded message. They could not. Even new Navajo recruits untrained in the code could not break it. Code Talkers could use the code because they were used to memorizing. Navajo songs and prayers are not written. They are kept alive orally—through spoken words.

Albert passed the testing. He had earned the right to wear the Code Talker uniform. Every part of his uniform stood for something larger. His red cap meant he was a Marine. His jewelry represented the Navajo. Light-colored pants stood for Mother Earth. Abalone-colored shoes stood for the sacred Navajo mountains.

Now Smith was in uniform and ready to fight. He was assigned to an infantry unit in the fourth Marine division based out of Maui, Hawaii. His first landing on an enemy-held beach came in the

Marshall Islands. What did he think as the boat splashed toward deadly gunfire? "No one thing. . . . Just scared," he said later. But he did what he had been trained to do. From 1943 to '45, he fought in four major battles: Marshall Islands, Saipan, Tarawa, and Iwo Jima.

Praise for the Code Talkers grew. One officer said, "Were it not for the Navajos, the Marines would never have taken Iwo Jima." The first two days of that battle, six Navajo code talkers worked around the clock. They sent and received over 800 error-free messages. The Japanese were skilled code breakers. But this code baffled them. On the morning of February 23, 1945, the American flag went up on the mountaintop. Victory!

Code Talkers faced more dangers than the usual horrors of war. They served 72-hour shifts behind enemy lines. They stayed within voice range of one other. The enemy could track radio activity. Not until the Code Talkers were back behind their own lines would they send radio messages.

Getting back through their own lines was not easy. Other American soldiers often mistook the Navajo for enemy soldiers and shot. Soon, bodyguards were assigned to each Code Talker. The bodyguards had secret orders to shoot Code Talkers if it looked like they would be captured. The military feared the code would fall into enemy hands.

August 15, 1945, was V-J Day. This stood for "Victory over Japan." The war in the Pacific Theater ended. Smith came home. He was not honored. None of the Code Talkers were. Tribal elders advised Smith to "leave the war behind." The Navajo culture values silence and balance. Telling war stories would go against both values. The government did not want

Code Talkers to tell war stories, either. They thought the code might be needed in the future. So the Navajo language was classified. The heroism of the Code Talkers was a state secret. Over 400 Code Talkers from the Navajo, Choctaw, Comanche, and Sioux nations were unsung heroes.

Smith went back to school. When he graduated, he could not find a job. So he joined the Army. After his discharge, he attended colleges in Colorado and New Mexico. He went on to work in elementary education for 40 years. In 1968, information about the Code Talkers was declassified. Smith could finally tell his wife of 47 years what he had done in the war.

Smith is now retired. He gives speeches about the Code Talkers. He helped make a Hollywood film, *Windtalkers*. He received a Congressional Medal of Honor. As one of his last official acts, President Clinton signed a bill granting these medals. At long last, the Code Talkers of World War II got the honor they deserved.

In 1982, Samantha Smith was 10. She was in the fifth grade and lived in Manchester, Maine. United States

President Ronald Reagan lived in the White House, in Washington, D.C. Yuri Andropov lived in Moscow. He had just become president of the Soviet Union.

Samantha got along with everyone. She liked roller-skating, reading, and playing with Kim, her Chesapeake Bay retriever. Presidents Reagan and Andropov did not get along. Each made nuclear weapons. Each promised he would never use his. This was the arms race of the Cold War.

Samantha worried that one president or the other would start a war. Other kids worried about that, too. So did adults.

Samantha was worried enough that winter to ask her mom to write to Andropov. Her mom said, "Why don't you?" So Samantha did. Here is part of her letter:

Congratulations on your new job. I have been worrying about Russia and the United States getting into a nuclear war. Are you going to have a war or not? If you aren't please tell me how you are going to not have a war. . . . God made the world for us to live together in peace and not fight.

She mailed her letter. Months passed. Then one April day, the principal called her to his office. Was she in trouble? No.

She had a phone call, that was all.

The caller was a reporter. He told Samantha that a newspaper in the Soviet Union had printed her letter. Amazing! Samantha did not know what to think.

Later that day, she wrote another letter to ask what was going on. She sent this one to the Soviet ambassador in Washington, D. C. The ambassador called her back a few days later. He told her to expect a letter from President Andropov.

Samantha and her father picked up the letter at the post office on April 25. Then they went home. Reporters crowded their front yard. They had heard about

Andropov's letter. They wanted to know what he had written.

The letter—more than two pages long—felt like it came "from a friend," Samantha said. Andropov called Samantha "a courageous and honest girl, resembling Becky, the friend of Tom Sawyer." He said no one in the Soviet Union wanted war. He invited Samantha and her parents to visit and see for themselves.

Were Samantha and her family being used for political purposes? *US News and World Report* magazine said they were. More press kept turning up at Samantha's home. There were reporters from *Time*,

Newsweek, public radio, *People*, NBC TV, and the Soviet press. Samantha found herself going to New York to be on the *Today Show*. Then she went to California to do the *Tonight Show*. Everyone wanted to know who she was and what she was up to. And most of all, would she accept Andropov's invitation?

Samantha and her family thought about it. Then they decided they would take the trip. In July, they toured the

Soviet Union for two weeks. They saw Moscow and Leningrad. They met the first woman in space, Valebtina Tereshkova. They ate burgers and fries with the U.S. ambassador. Samantha spent several days at a Soviet youth camp. She stayed in a dormitory with nine other girls. These girls worried about nuclear war, too.

Was the trip propaganda, meant to send a message? "I suppose there might be something in that," Samantha's father said when they got home. But, he went on, the Soviets had something to lose, too. The U.S.S.R. could not hide what was really going on inside it. His family had met people who talked openly about problems such as food shortages. These problems were caused by the money spent on the arms race.

Not all American military intelligence officers thought the Soviet Union was a threat. The Soviets had done things the United States did not like in the past, but their country was weaker now. These officers said the fear that fueled the Cold War was misplaced.

But this did not stop criticism of Samantha's trip. The criticism did not stop Samantha, either. She still asked *why* U.S. and Soviet leaders went on making weapons when people in both countries wanted peace.

By now, she was famous. Audiences wanted to listen to her. She juggled speeches and appearances with her usual life. She wrote a book, *Journey to the Soviet Union*. She and her mother attended the Children's International Symposium in Kobe, Japan. There she met the Japanese prime minister. At the symposium, she spoke out for peace. She hosted a Disney television special during the 1984 presidential campaign. The special taught kids about the candidates, politics, and the government. Then Hollywood called. Would Samantha star in *Lime Street*, a television series? If so, she would play actor Robert Wagner's daughter. Samantha said she would.

In August 1985, Samantha finished a segment of *Lime Street* in London. She and her father flew back to Maine. Their plane missed the runway and crashed into the woods. Everyone on board was killed. Samantha was only 13.

In the following years, the Soviets issued a stamp in Samantha's honor. They named a diamond, a flower, a mountain, and a planet after her. President Andropov lost power. The Soviet Union broke up into smaller countries, including Russia. President Reagan's term ran out.

Samantha's home state erected a bronze statue of her at the State Library. The statue shows her releasing a dove. A bear cub stands at her side. The bear is a symbol of both Maine and Russia. In her short life, Samantha made a lasting impression on many people.

Millions of people around the world are poor. They are so poor that if they had to buy air, they would die in two minutes. That is how long people can live without breathing.

In 1982 in Pakistan, a couple this poor had a son. Their name was Masih. They named their baby Iqbal. Four years later, their daughter, Sobia, was born. Now Iqbal's mother needed an operation. Where would the money come from? Could they sell something? What did they have that anyone would buy?

They had Iqbal. Many very poor parents sell their children as bonded laborers. In reality, these children are debt slaves.

A carpet factory owner loaned Iqbal's

parents money for the operation. In return, Iqbal would work for him. He would work 12 hours a day—more, when business was good. Iqbal's wages, pennies a day, would repay the loan. Debt slaves can be sold to other owners. Iqbal ended up as the property of Arshad Ghullah.

Iqbal joined the other kids in Ghullah's rug factory. They squatted at looms and tied knots in carpets. The fibers made their hands bleed. They accidentally cut themselves with carpet knives. If they fell asleep, they were beaten with a rug fork. There was no lunch period and no recess. Sometimes workers did not behave as the owners liked. Then factory owners could tie their ankles and hang them upside down. That would bring them back in line.

Years went by. Iqbal's back curved because he got no exercise. He did not grow much. His lungs weakened from breathing carpet dust. His fingers were twisted. And he longed for freedom!

Then his half-brother got engaged to be married. His family needed a sack of sugar and some grain to prepare for the wedding. Gullah loaned them more money. He added it to Iqbal's debt. Now Iqbal's debt was 13,000 rupees ($250 American). He would never earn enough to buy his freedom, he told his sister.

Life at the carpet factory was grim. Sometimes Iqbal and his friends needed a break. Then they would wait until Ghullah was gone. They would tell the foreman they were going to throw up. The foreman did not want vomit on the carpets. The children were allowed to leave. Freedom! The kids would play all day.

But the next morning, Ghullah would find them. He took them to the factory and beat them. He chained them to their looms. Their parents were allowed to bring food. They had to. Ghullah would keep the children working for as long as he could. Once he kept them for two days.

Then Iqbal heard wonderful news. There was a new law against debt slavery in Pakistan! The Bonded Labour Abolition Act gave him the right to leave work! One October morning in 1992, he did. He was 10 now. He joined other child and adult debt slaves on a wagon. An hour later, they were at a meeting of the BLLF (Bonded Labour Liberation Front).

The BLLF leader, Ehsan Ullah Khan, spoke. He saw Iqbal in the audience. Afterwards, Ehsan talked with Iqbal.

Ehsan asked Iqbal to speak to the group. Iqbal hesitated. But finally he did.

The next day at work, Ghullah was furious with Iqbal. And Ehsan worried about him. If only Iqbal could come to a BLLF school! Then Ehsan had his chance. Iqbal and his mother came to BLLF headquarters. Ehsan asked if Iqbal wanted to go to school. Yes! Iqbal's mother agreed. The boy would live at the school and come home on visits.

School was great! Iqbal went to a school party, something he had never done before. And there were more new things. Children from Sweden visited his school.

Iqbal made new friends. He learned easily and became a good speaker. He told children in the carpet factories they did not need to stay with their owners. First hundreds, then thousands of children quit. This upset the owners. Some, like Ghullah, filed false claims with the police. Ghullah said Iqbal and the other children stole from him. He said they threatened him with weapons.

In 1994 Ehsan asked Iqbal another important question. Did he want to go to Sweden to visit his friends there? Yes! But there was a problem—there was no evidence that Iqbal existed. There were no papers, such as a birth certificate, that proved who Iqbal was. Many poor people in Pakistan are "invisible" like this. But this could be fixed. Then Iqbal had other good news. He had won a prize in the United States! The prize was for his work in freeing over 3,000 children from debt slavery. After five weeks in Sweden, Iqbal flew to the U.S. to receive his award. There, he was also named "Person of the Week" on ABC news.

Then Iqbal went back to school. He continued his efforts to help other children. He made plans to visit his mother and sister at Easter. When Easter 1995 came, Iqbal went home. The carpet factory owners knew he would.

On Easter morning, Iqbal went to church. That evening, he visited his relatives, Lyaqat and Faryad Masih. All three rode on the same bicycle to take food to Lyagat's father who was working in his field. It was dark. Halfway to the field, Iqbal was shot and killed. The other boys had minor injuries. A fieldhand was arrested for the murder. He was threatened with death if he told what really happened.

That is how the story stood until 1999. That was when a Swedish film, *Death of the Slaveboy,* revealed the truth. Two men believed to be murderers had told the police the fieldworker was the killer.

Carpet factory owners backed them up. The boys with Iqbal who had seen the murder knew better.

Now the killers threaten these boys. They threaten Iqbal's mother and sister, too. Iqbal is dead, but his story still lives. His heroic struggle is not yet finished.

Ruby Bridges, In a Class by Herself

On November 14, 1960, Ruby Bridges was six years old. She had a new outfit because she was going to a new school in

New Orleans. "Behave yourself today, Ruby," her mom said, "and don't be afraid. There might a lot of people outside this new school, but I'll be with you."

Then a car full of federal marshals pulled up. They drove Ruby and her mom to William Frantz Elementary. It was only five blocks away from where Ruby Bridges lived. Ruby's old school was a lot farther away than that. On the way, the marshals told them how to get out of the car and how to walk into school. Stay behind two of us, the marshals said, and in front of two others.

Outside the school, Ruby saw people

throwing things and shouting. She thought it might be Mardi Gras. People partying during Mardi Gras acted like that. Ruby, her mom, and the marshals got out and walked through the screaming crowd. Once inside the school, they went to the principal's office. For the first time, Ruby had an inkling that something unusual was going on. Through glass doors, she saw angry white parents rushing around with their kids. They shouted and pointed at Ruby and her mom.

Something unusual *was* going on. A federal court had ordered the New Orleans school system to desegregate. Ruby would be the first African American enrolled in

William Frantz Elementary.

It had started the spring before. All the city's black kindergarteners had taken a test. The results would determine who would go to an integrated school. Ruby was one of six kids chosen. Her mother thought Ruby would get a better education if she went to the new school. A good education would lead to a good job later in life. Ruby's father did not agree. He thought it was "just asking for trouble." But Ruby's mom convinced her dad that they had to take this step for all black children.

So now Ruby was here, in this new school. She spent her whole first day sitting with her mom in the principal's office. They could not go to class because of the uproar. The next day, the crowd was back. Ruby saw a black doll in a coffin. That scared her more than what the people said.

The marshals took them to a first-grade classroom. Ruby's teacher was there. Desks were there. But there were no kids. Ruby thought she was early. She did not know the school had been boycotted. The other kids were being kept at home.

Her teacher, Mrs. Henry, was white. It was the first time Ruby had had a white teacher. She was nervous. The angry crowd was white, too. But Mrs. Henry seemed nice. She asked Ruby to pick a seat, then sat down beside her. She began teaching the alphabet.

The third day, Ruby's mother did not go to school with Ruby and the marshals. She had work and other children to look after. But she told Ruby, "Remember, if you get afraid, say your prayers. You can pray to God any time, anywhere." So Ruby began a practice of praying in the marshals' car on the way to school. And at school, every day for a year, it was the same—just Ruby and Mrs. Henry.

The classroom was a safe haven. Outside, angry mobs marched. There were riots. Ruby's father was fired from his job. Her grandparents, sharecroppers in Mississippi, were asked to move. But letters of support and donations came in from around the country. A neighbor gave her dad work. Other neighbors baby-sat or watched the Bridgeses' house to stop troublemakers. Some neighbors even walked behind the marshals' car as it drove Ruby to school.

Ruby could not go outside for recess because of the protestors. So Mrs. Henry stayed in with her. They played games and did jumping jacks to music. Ruby thought that Mrs. Henry proved the truth of Dr. Martin Luther King, Jr.'s lesson: Never judge people by the color of their skins. She came to love and trust Mrs. Henry. She even picked up her teacher's Boston accent.

Once Ruby forgot to say her prayers until she was in the middle of the mob. She stopped and prayed right then and there. Mrs. Henry, watching from a window, saw Ruby's lips move. Later, Mrs. Henry asked what she'd been saying. Ruby said, "I wasn't talking to them. I was praying for them." The hug Mrs. Henry gave Ruby then was nice. The proud expression on her face was even better.

The school year ended. Summer came and went. Ruby did not need a marshal when she returned to school in September. There were no angry crowds. And there were other kids in her second-grade class. There were even some black kids.

But something was not right. Mrs. Henry was not there. She had not been hired back. She and her husband had moved back to Boston. It took a while to get used to. But then Ruby was ready to go on. She finished grade school, then high school, then business school. She worked before marrying, then raised four sons. When her brother died, she helped raise his daughters. The girls attended William Frantz. Ruby—now Ruby Bridges Hall—began volunteering at the same school she had helped to integrate. She also started the Ruby Bridges Foundation. She hoped to persuade parents to take a more active role in their children's education.

And Mrs. Henry? The two met more

than 35 years after their year together. Mrs. Henry said, "You know, it's funny, I just realized that neither one of us ever missed a day of school." Ruby replied, "You're right. I don't know what we would have done."

Today, they speak together at schools around the country. Their friendship is proof of Ruby Bridges Hall's belief that "schools can be a place to bring people together."

Many people do not like housework. Brown Weasel Woman was one of them.

She was born after her people first owned horses and rifles, but before white settlers came to her land. Her tribe was Pikuni, which means "The Real People." White settlers called them Blackfeet because the bottoms of their moccasins were dyed or stained black. The Pikuni and their allies were a great military power. They controlled much of the northwestern Great Plains.

Brown Weasel Woman was her mother's first child. Everybody thought she would grow up to do women's work. Part of that job would be taking charge of the tipi. This meant more than keeping the dwelling clean. It meant taking the tipi down, packing it, moving it, and putting it back up again whenever the family moved. And families moved often. They followed the buffalo. She would also gather roots and berries—anything that was not meat. She would bear children and raise them. She would cook. She would sew her family's clothes. She would decorate the clothes for special occasions with dyed quills and beads. She would tan the hides of buffalo and other animals men brought back from the hunt.

By the time Brown Weasel Woman had two brothers and two sisters, she knew a few things. She knew how to do women's work. She also knew she would rather do something else. She asked her father to make her a bow and arrow. He taught her to use them. She learned so fast that she was soon going on buffalo hunts.

Buffalo, or bison, was essential for the hunting tribes' survival. Bison skins were made into tipis and warm robes. Spoons and other utensils were made from bison bones. Their meat was food. But hunting bison was not easy. Male bison, or bulls, weigh 1,800 pounds. The average weight of a female, or cow, is half a ton. A bison measures about 6 feet from shoulder to ground. Despite their bulk, huge bison can move fast. A hunter who fell under their running hooves would probably be killed.

So hunters approached bison herds carefully. They came on one horse, then switched to a swift, sure-footed horse. This horse was called "a buffalo runner." The hunters rode into the herd with their bows and arrows. Why not rifles? It is hard to reload while riding bareback on a galloping horse. Also, an arrow's markings told which hunter could claim which bison.

Brown Weasel Woman was not just along for the ride. She claimed her share of bison. And she acted bravely in other ways. During one hunt, her group met an enemy war party. Her father's horse was shot out from under him. Brown Weasel

Woman turned back, picked up her father, and brought him back to their village. That was one of the bravest things a warrior could do.

People began to wonder what made Brown Weasel Woman tick. Why didn't she act like a woman? Village elders told her to go on a vision quest. Before, only men had been allowed to do this. She would go to a lonely place. She would not eat for four days. Instead, she would pray and seek dreams, or visions. These would reveal her medicine, her true path in life. Some men did this and failed.

Brown Weasel Woman sought her vision above a waterfall in what is now Glacier National Park. She succeeded. Her vision told her to keep doing what she was doing. The Spirit World had given her special powers. After that, no one questioned her behavior.

She became the head of her family when her parents died. A widowed woman moved in to do the housework. Brown Weasel Woman remained on the warrior path. She hunted and protected her family. She rode on raids and with war parties.

She joined a war party against the

Crows, who had raided the Pikuni's horses. Brown Weasel Woman stole back 11 horses. Other warriors in the party reclaimed the rest. They started back to their camp. It was a long ride away. Brown Weasel Woman stood watch on the top of a butte during a rest. Two enemy warriors approached. One had a rifle. Brown Weasel Woman ran down the butte with her rifle. She grabbed the lead horse's rope to keep the rest of the herd from running.

The enemy warriors kept coming. They had seen she was a woman. They did not think they would have any trouble. But they should have thought twice.

Brown Weasel Woman shot the one carrying the rifle. Shooting both her rifle and his, she chased the others away.

Once she joined a war party planning to capture horses from a tribe over the Rocky Mountains. They took more than 600 horses. Brown Weasel Woman was shot at but not hurt. She was drawing more and more attention.

That summer, the allied tribes gathered as they usually did. The get-together was partly social and partly business. During Medicine Lodge ceremonies, warriors stood and told of their brave deeds. Brown Weasel Woman was asked to stand with them. She spoke, and people clapped. Then more honor came. The head chief gave her a new name—Pi'tamaka, or Running Eagle. It was the name of earlier famous warriors. This had never been done for a woman.

She became a member of the Braves Society of young warriors. She was allowed to sing their songs, dance their dances, and wear their regalia—ceremonial clothes and jewelry. She was someone to be reckoned with. Then, during a battle, Running Eagle was clubbed from behind and killed.

Memory of the woman warrior did not

die. She became one of the most famous women in Blackfoot history. The site of her vision quest above a waterfall is still sacred to her people. Originally, the place was called Pi'tamaka Falls. The Park Service later changed the name to Trick Falls and put in hiking trails. But Pi'tamaka/Running Eagle had forged her own trails. She was a hero.

Colombia, a country in South America, has serious problems. It is rich in oil, gold, silver, and coal deposits. But it is also rich in war. Conflict is never-ending. Ordinary, innocent people often get caught in the crossfire.

War has taken the homes of over two million Colombians. More than half the homeless are kids. Many of these kids end up fighting in the war. Some kids want to fight. Others are kidnapped and forced into battle. Both sides use anti-personnel mines—explosive devices. The mines kill about 200 people every year. Forty percent of the victims are kids.

One child decided to change this. His name is Gerson Andres Florez Perez. When he was 10, he took an unusual vacation. He visited some Colombian villages where people died every day. At first he wanted to see these places out of curiosity. Then he started meeting other kids. He made friends.

Back at home 15 days later, he saw a shocking television news report. Mines had killed two of his new friends. That is when he decided to help young victims of these weapons and to fight against their use.

This may sound like an impossible job for a 10-year-old. But Gerson analyzed what he had to do to reach his goal. He had to attract the public's attention. He also had to make an impact on the government and the media. This would not be easy. But he had the support of his parents and friends.

In June 1997, he wrote a proposal in simple, straightforward language. He called it "Children of Peace." He was not demanding or pushy. He was polite but determined. The media listened. Gerson says it was easy to get their attention because he was the first child to talk publicly about such things. People whose job is to get media attention say their work is hard. Sometimes it is impossible. But Gerson managed to get his thoughts to a wide audience.

Then he managed some other "impossible" things. He spoke to the Colombian National Congress. He asked them to adopt the Treaty of Ottawa. This treaty banned mines worldwide. Others supported him. Later, his country signed the treaty.

Gerson was proud of helping to make that happen. He was even more proud of something else. His speech opened the door for other Colombian children to speak out, he says. It was the first time anyone as young as he spoke to the

Colombian Congress.

In the past few years, Gerson has seen other "impossible" things happen. Programs geared to children's needs have been started. His speeches for children's rights have led him to powerful people. He has met with three Latin American presidents, Queen Noor of Jordan, and representatives of peace groups such as World Voices. He has met with children in other countries around the world. He has also met with the men who kill kids. That last meeting took place deep in a jungle. Gerson knew he might not come out.

Gerson does more than talk. He has

contributed writings to books. Books about his work for peace have been published. He wrote a song, "Constructores de Paz," or "Peace Builders." The Philharmonic orchestras of Bogota and Oslo recorded it. Gerson hoped that sale of the CDs would help pay medical expenses for children injured by mines.

It has. In July 2001, a mine exploded under eight-year-old Luis Alejandro. The blast destroyed both his legs. They were amputated. His family was poor. They could not buy the artificial limbs or the therapy Luis needed to learn to use them. The government would not help. Money from CD sales of Gerson's song did.

This is not the first time Gerson sold things to support his work. He peddled buttons for six weeks to cover travel expenses to The Hague Appeal Conference for Peace. By now, he has gained much media attention. He has won awards including the National Peace Award. And—impossibly!—he and the Children's Movement for Peace were Nobel Peace Prize nominees.

Gerson is not after fame. The real issue is peace. Real peace.

"Peace isn't the absence of war," Gerson says. He has gone beyond simple answers like that. Lack of food or work also leads to violence. He pictures a nonviolent world, where kids have chances to dream and play. He works to help make that happen.

He also allows himself time to play. He plays the guitar. He likes football and surfing the Net. And he loves salsa dancing. He says, "At age three, you listen to the music, at age five, you watch people dancing and by age 15, it's like you've been dancing always."

In January 2002, Perez became the youngest law student at the University of New Granada in Bogota. He began classes

. . . and went on with his work for peace. He had meetings with kids in the poorest parts of Bogota. Violence is a way of life in these areas of the city. In October 2002, he was attacked and stabbed. By whom? Why? No one knows. Doctors told his family that the wounds would take time to heal.

In the meantime, the seeds of his vision have been planted. Who knows what can flower?

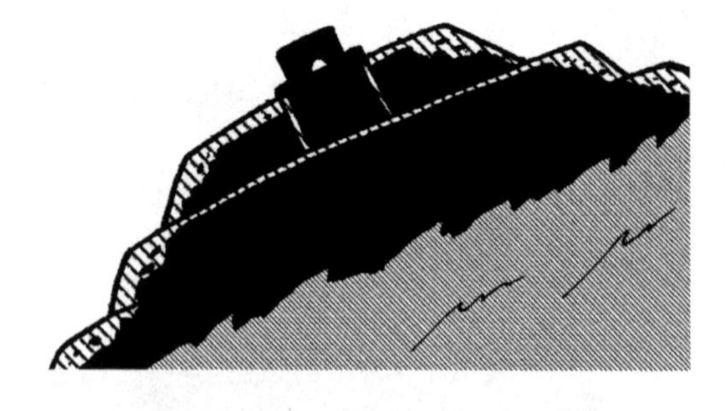